On the Back of the Wind

FRANK DULLAGHAN

Cinnamon Press
Independent Innovative International

Published by Cinnamon Press
Meirion House
Glan yr afon
Tanygrisiau
Blaenau Ffestiniog,
Gwynedd
LL41 3SU
www.cinnamonpress.com

The right of Frank Dullaghan to be identified as author of this work has been asserted by him in accordance with the Copyright, Designs and Patent Act, 1988. Copyright © 2008 Frank Dullaghan. ISBN: 978-1-905614-47-9
British Library Cataloguing in Publication Data. A CIP record for this book can be obtained from the British Library.

Designed and typeset in Palatino by Cinnamon Press. Cover design by Mike Fortune-Wood from original artwork by Aidan Dullaghan B.A. (fine arts) *On the Back of the Wind*, oil on canvas 150cm x 10cm © Aidan Dullaghan, used with kind permission.
Printed by Biddles Ltd, Norfolk

Acknowledgements:

Some of these poems, or earlier versions of them, have appeared in the following places: *The Dark Horse; Dubai Irish Society 2007 Annual; Equinox; First Pressings* (Faber & Faber); *The Honest Ulsterman; London Magazine; Magma; New Poetry Ventures website; The New Welsh Review; Nimrod* (USA); *Orbis; Poetry London; Poetry Review: Poetry Wales; Poets for Oxfam CDs The Printer's Devil; Quadrant* (Australia); *Reactions; The Rialto; The Shop; Smiths Knoll; Teaching a Chicken to Swim* (Seren Press); *Thumbscrew; Verse; and Wordplay.* Thanks to The Art Council's New Talent Scheme for a grant that allowed this collection to be gathered together and to Stephen Knight for working with me in shaping the collection and for his close reading of the poems. Thanks also to Anne Berkeley for her close reading of a number of these poems.

Biography:

Frank Dullaghan was born in Dundalk, Ireland, and read Economics at University College Dublin. He also holds an MA with Distinction in Creative Writing from Glamorgan University. He was one of the main organisers of the *Essex Poetry Festival* and led the panel of judges for the *Young Essex Poet of the Year* competition. For many years, Frank also edited *Seam* poetry journal. In September 2006 he moved to Dubai with Libertas Capital Group plc, a small international investment banking company he co-founded in 2002. Frank has been a keen martial artist and holds a black belt in Judo, a top brown belt in Karate and a senior grade in Wing Tsun Kung Fu. He is married with two adult sons.

Contents

For my wife, Marie,
and my sons, Fergus and Aidan

— the pen is mightier than the soup spoon.

On the Back of the Wind

Chesterfield Road

Not so much the two years of my life tucked up behind me
nor the room I will learn to reconstruct in my head

nor the rain softening this late afternoon light
as if something is about to begin,

not even that quarter circle of wear on the carpet
I notice now for the first time, as I pull the door closed,

nor the way the paintwork glimmers –
a thing remembered, then lost – when the door is forced

through the arc of its stiffness. It is more the steps
leading down to the footpath, the weight of the hedge,

the way the gate clicks itself closed, keeps its counsel,
you brushing your hair in another part of the city.

My Niece Takes Me on a Journey

For Shannon

Look, she says, and offers the drawing.
Who is it? It's you, silly.
And of course she's right. It is me.
There I am with one leg longer than the other
going for that big step forward,
my purple eyes lopsided with the effort,
a manic yellow grin, and my arms wide
as a tightrope walker's. *And this?*
She looks at me and shakes her head.
My car? I recognise it now,
the green box of it balanced on two wheels,
hovering under my left armpit,
its lights on, its journey waiting.

Eden

He came in through the sliding doors and sat,
not bothering with the empty seat –
like a missing tooth in the full compartment –
but settled himself down in the passageway,
his rucksack by his side.

When I looked up again, he had a frying pan out,
a small camping stove hissing like a snake.
I watched as he buttered the pan – two tablespoons –
placed a sausage, snipped from its fellows
with a small penknife attached to his key-ring.

Half the carriage was back at their breakfast tables,
Saturday, their suits hanging dark and unfilled.
He opened a Tupperware box, took out one rasher –
back bacon, rind removed – laid it
like an offering and turned the sausage to brown.

He cracked an egg. It whitened and spat.
The shells he dropped into a small paper bag
in his pocket. Even those deep in the well
of their sleep, murmured and stirred.

It was mother and childhood, unspoiled ease,
the indulgence of Mt. Ararat when Noah stepped out
of the Ark, as if returned to the Garden of Eden,
and all of his words taking flight.

Arrow

For Mary

It was one of those hot summers, '65 probably. I made arrows
from reeds that grew along the back of our terrace gardens.
I had been shown by a boy at school, how to squeeze a one-inch nail
into the soft head of the reed, just above one of those knuckles
in its thin unbending finger, how to wedge it in and bind it.
I was spending the afternoon sending my arrows from a bow
into the open mouth of a target I had chalked
on the back of the coal-house door. I was good. My score was high
and my technique – which I was imagining as if I were a onlooker,
part of the crowd gasping as Robin Hood uncloaked himself
with his mastery at that famous tournament long ago – was excellent.
Each arrow thunked itself solidly into the door's timber and trembled.
It was then that my sister came out, with her round face,
her dolls, all her girl stuff, and stood in the shadow of my skill.
I'll tell, she said. We both knew I'd been told to stop,
to leave that door alone, that arrows were dangerous.
I'll tell. And we both knew that she would.
I turned. I notched an arrow, bent the bow. *You'd better not!*
I was in a green forest, my band of men watching.
My sister was on the Sheriff's side. *You'd better not.*
The air held its breath for a soft moment. Birds were quiet.
She turned to run – *Mammy!* – towards the house.
The arrow flashed from the bow, making its own tunnel through the air.
It sank into her chest. I saw a trout speared from a river,
its cry a sliver of light. As she ran the shaft danced up and down
until it lost its grip, fell and was kicked away by her running feet.
And still, it is not the doom that came upon me
but the way the arrow danced, that lives.

Riding Off Into the Sunset

He might have been,
as they'd have said
in one of those early American films,
a *Jock*, or as my boss, much later,
in an American investment bank, would say,
a *Big Swinging Dick*.
But neither he nor I were American

And he was, anyway,
more of what my father would have called
a *Corner Boy*.
But whatever it was he was,
it would seem that you liked it –
that dangerous edge that he had,
that promise of something

that wasn't quite pain
and wasn't quite not,
so that when I called for you,
you were gone – out on the back of his bike,
calling him *Baby, Baby*
as he hurtled the two of you
round the bends and into the setting sun.

The Interview

This is where the money's made – Wall Street, Broad Street,
New York Plaza. The buildings tilt your head back.

I've come to be interviewed for a job in London.
Flown in for the day, as if the people here have some gift,

of knowledge or benediction, that is worth the cost.
I'd lifted off at Heathrow, watched

as the airport shrunk to a microchip.
The cloud-top was a white cauliflower forest that darkened

as the night came on and the full moon gaped
above its fuzzy image, could not drop through.

Perhaps when you're that high, it's hard
to reflect upon the ground. I take the elevator up.

Offices with space and an unequalled view – Liberty, Ellis Island.
Here it is – opportunity, a figure rising from behind a desk.

A Walk in a Field

For Thomas

I remember you telling it –
home from the Leb, wife in the other room –
how your friend stepped on a mine,

how he froze, knowing not to move,
his scarecrow shadow stretching
while you followed your footprints back

to gather rocks, piled them round his feet
adding pressure, back and forth,
each placed gently like gifts for a king

until the second click gave warning –
seconds to move: sprinting, shouting,
diving as the ground ripped open,
the world folding over you, raining.

What am I Bid

for this watch, this belt, these shoes, this half-used notebook
    with its promise not yet filled, this pen that bears
    my company's name, this loose fist of change.

for this business plan, this strategy, this team
    who boot the share price up, this logo, this office desk,
    these late nights polishing numbers until they shine like stars.

for the clunk of this door, the steel wrapped about me, a space pod,
    the smell of leather sprayed in the air, the MG badge, the stereo,
    the AA roadmap of the galaxy on the back seat.

for this exhaustion, this emptiness of effort, the blue sea of the *tatami*
    swaying under me, my *judogi's* damp fabric cooling, brown belt
    spilling, my new black belt's rigid coil looped in my hand.

for the way the raucous rush of the school corridor submerges
    into some place else, the now of this sheet of paper
    filling me up like a shout.

for this winter alley, these high hedges, her cold nose
    against my neck as she bites me, my hand under her coat,
    warming on her breast.

for this furious race of flame in our Christmas grate, Daddy's
    satisfaction, the pudding that has swung in its greased cloth
    between the legs of his chair for the past week.

for this negation of next, this impossible now, this self that is
    no longer self, this last breath's birth,
    this poem hammered onto the page.

Speed of Dark

His death is curled beside him in his bed,
an old dog in from the cold.
It seems he's grown comfortable
with its rasp and wheeze, its sudden shudders.

The TV, his source of noise,
can no longer stop his eyes from closing.
Outside, the world has turned away
like darkness chasing the last of light

when a star explodes, moving
first at the same speed, then its own.
The clock on his wall tenders its tick
to the deepening pool of the room.

But there are no purchasers of time here
where the currency is softly changing.
The old man goes time travelling.
The dog settles down.

Recovery Ward

This is the hand
    that laid each brick,
    that levelled the risers
    stepping the stairs,
    that made the door fast
    against the world,
    that ruled with a grip
    tight as terror.

This is the hand
    that fisted the heart,
    that brooked no excuse
    but always found fault
    in its hunger to hit,
    that lifted the leg –
    that it broke from the chair –
    to his daughter.

This is the hand
    that's been stopped by a clot
    that lies broken-backed
    on a crisp clean sheet,
    that he strokes like a cat
    he's trying to wake.
    He should leave it for dead.
    It is better.

Starbucks

The morning is dark
till she stirs in the milk,
shakes in some sweetness.

This is where she pauses each morning,
holding the small moment of coffee,
sipping at its stillness.

When she steps back into the moving world,
she walks with her back straight,
looks neither right nor left,

the flap of her long hair
like a scream behind her,
her silence, in front, like a knife.

The Silence

You can wear your silence like a room.
It will not stop you feeling lonely.

Look how your moon has cracked its head,
its light is pooling in the lake.

Your sky has lost all sense of where it's going,
its stars are overheating fast.

The fence that you have built to keep him out
throws shadows on your garden.

He walks street by street away, is destitute.
You can feel the silence harden.

Under the Roof

High up under the roof, the ceiling slices down
over the central rug, where you can stand to dress,

dance in a straight line or just gaze out of the attic window
across a regiment of roofs, houses standing shoulder to shoulder,

their long gardens separated by a wall or fence, horizontal streaks
stepping up into the grey evening, the blot of a shed here and there

like knots in the grain of wood. The bed is low on the floor.
You could wedge yourself into sleep or sit on its outer edge

to read in the last of the light. Or step onto the stairs
that falls back down into the house and knock yourself out

on the cross-beam in the dark, trying to make it to the bathroom,
kitchen, phone. But instead, just lie on your back

listening to the building – the gargle of its pipes, the chattering
of its windows to the wind. Lie there on your back,

under the rim of the roof, wonder at the dark universe
with its billion suns, each of them warming their own small worlds,

falling away from you as dreams rush in and the names
of old lovers get confused with the names of the dead.

Ferryman

The ferry line swung in a long arc over the river.
It was old, basic, the boat attached by a loop
that the ferryman slipped along the line, pulled down on,

hauling us across, to sit in the sun with our pints.
Then, in that way that a crowd lifts its head, we looked up,
saw a young man out on the line, crawling

leg over leg for a bet, crossing back to the pier.
Half-way over his arms hung straight. We were sure he was gone.
But he stayed, hand-grab to hand-grab

on the long pull up from the centre to the other side.
Both banks broke into cheers and the ferryman jerked his boat
into movement, crossing over the water after him.

This is how it should be: surprising yourself, being able
to stand on the far shore with your arms crossed,
resting, taking the applause, waiting for the ferryman.

The Royal Academy

I'm taking my poem to be judged at the Royal Academy.
I'm taking it on the train. It's here on the seat beside me

wrapped in brown paper. Originally, I'd intended something large.
But that's been done so well, anything now would be a poor copy.

The train lurches through the suburbs – back gardens all stain and grime,
washed-out ochres, smoky greys. My poem sits quietly.

Perspective and composition have given way to ideas.
I'm taking the idea of my poem to be judged at the Royal Academy.

I've been thinking about it, here in the train beside me,
touching it up as the train enters into the dream

of backyards and walls, windows curtained with newspapers,
words catching the sun behind glass, browning.

It's always the dream that we want. I'm taking the dream of my poem
to the Royal Academy as the train leaves the tracks

and the houses gather up their lean-tos and sheds, their rusting bikes,
and peel away from the carriage window. We're together

as the sky rushes down and cloud presses its dead-flesh palms
to the glass. I'm being taken to the Royal Academy.

Dressed in brown paper, I'm holding something
tight and small, like a word not yet written.

I'm holding something for the judges. I'm holding something
that will subvert the walls of the Royal Academy.

Doing P8 in Winter

We were wet from the start, squeezing in
where the stream splashed down,

damming the flow with our back and shoulders,
plunging into the throat of the cave.

We went with the flow, belly-crawling,
fingers kneading the rock's muddy skin,

before standing into lamp-shoved shadows,
watching walls convulse about us.

Our voices stayed close. Our minds adjusted to the dark.
I watched you hold yourself tight,

telling no one your terror at confinement
as you unravelled yourself from a cut in the rock.

We went deeper, legs arching walls, hands on the roof,
as water routed its own way below,

the light from our helmet lamps nodded
and swept into halls like scatter-brained ghosts.

We came to where a weight of water fell, gushed down,
showered the pool far below in a rush of sound,

Then we too went down,
Abseiling into that roar, flopping through the pool

to spill onto spray-slicked slabs, humped
like great seals in the wavering eyes of our lamps.

We went even deeper, until water finally stopped us,
lying there at our feet in black silence,

wide and deep and without marvel.
Peeled half-out of wet suits we pissed at its edge

before turning back. Levering ourselves through the rocks
we fought the water's plunge to rise,

one slow foot at a time, up a steel rope ladder,
till our hands froze to claws and cold sliced into our skin.

Then hand-over-hand we climbed out,
our muscles wet on our bones, to stand

under a darkening sky, no walls to the world,
stars giddy above us and wind ripping water from our eyes.

Seeing the Light

How sophisticated these girls are,
thirteen or fourteen years old,
sitting in this coffee shop eating pastries,
conspiring together with their dark eyes
so that everyone else here feels like outsiders.
I swear to God, one says in her South Kerry lilt.
And whatever it is she attests to
they all bubble into laughter.

I broke the surface of the book I was reading,
to take notice of them – full of themselves
the way most of us are empty of ourselves,
throwing their light about this room
like they had batteries to spare,
globules of it landing on tables
where old men mutter to newspapers,
where a woman checks that she hasn't changed
in a little pocket mirror.

And one globule touches down on my table
between my poetry book and the salt cellar,
sits there pulsing, excited by its own luminance.
It would seem that I'm the only one to notice.
The girls have no regard,
incandescent as they are in their high voltage,
the only impossibility the old men believe in
is their own, and the young woman
reflects only on herself.

I pick up my gift
and place it on my tongue,
looking for that particular wisdom of youth
that would make everything possible again.

Homecoming

For Marie

On the long night road
is where you'll be,
drumming through darkness,
an envelope of light,
the children keeled to sleep
in the back.

In the wide light of my room
I listen to the sing
of night, the unnoise
as much in my head
as outside, waiting the *shhhh*
of the gravel,

anticipating the shot
of a car door shut,
the commotion of roused children,
a stumble of bags,
your voice meeting mine
on the stairs.

Lift-Off

I lifted off,
the row of houses
like a stalled convoy
of articulated lorries,
the woods pressing their posies
of rust and flame
into the green hills.
I lifted till the sea curved
to the mould of the earth
and the earth was a gift
half-unwrapped
from its package of cloud.
I was my own elevator
to the stars,
fast as a heart
climbing to its climax,
my head full of journey
and the sun hammering
through the dark centres
of my eyes.

Weight

I'm gaining weight. I used to be ten stone.
I weigh fourteen in my *Doc Martens* now.
My friends say it's depression, some unknown
disease, a change of climate, stress or how
my stars fall. Still I feel I'm bursting through
my shirts. New suits from *High & Mighty* stores
are not far off and some house spending's due –
for one, I'll have to reinforce the floors.

Of course, I know what they will never know –
that this is a reaction of the heart
that fills itself with hope that's hard to hide.
A glance or touch in passing makes it grow
to weigh me down, add stones. Soon it will start
ballooning to your smile. It's suicide.

Kawasaki

It's the way the roofs caught fire
in the morning sun or the way fields
along the Castletown Road
flooded into green just after dawn.
It's what I expected – the coin
flipped to land on its tail,
the dice tumbled each time to a two,
the wishbone holding onto its handle.
But when Kevin unzipped your street
with his Kawasaki, parted
St. Nicholas' Avenue like a comb
through his hair, showed you the straight
line out, the roads beyond
Ard Easmunn, Seatown, Bridge-a-Crinn,
when he opened the map of the possible
that lay beyond the roads I walked,
you were gone.
                              I cannot say when, Mary, exactly.
But perhaps it was leaning into a corner,
the hedgerows streaking the sky
and the sun setting its palm
between his shoulder blades
where your cheek may have touched the dark
of his leathers. And perhaps then, too,
I was seated as usual
on a shuddering train, ready to move
out of Connelly Street Station,
coming home for the weekend,
my university books in my bag,
expecting everything the same – no more
than you on the platform to meet me,
no less than believing
that the world started and stopped at your door.

Her Hair like a River

For Marie

She ran down Grafton Street to meet me,
stopped half-way and pulled up her socks,
the wind whipped up her red hair
and she smiled.

She smiled out at me and she laughed at me.
For I was home from England,
we were getting married that weekend,
stepping out into the world together.

The wind whipped up her red hair,
spreading light across the street,
spreading light onto the washed doorstep
of that big city shop

where she knelt for a moment on the footpath,
her knee gleaming in the sun
till she let her skirt fall back down,
standing up again –

to run down Grafton Street and greet me,
her hair out behind her like a river,
her arms opening up to drown me,
the sun forever on her face.

The Fisherman's Tale

I stole her from the ocean,
her wet breasts salty to my lips.
I rode her astride, watching her moon-eyes fill
as her tail trumped and thrashed beneath me.
She cried like a gull,
her hands beating my back.

I took her home, kept the door locked,
came back in the evenings
with my arms full of fish.
She got used to it,
slowly losing her sheen,
touch of green in her hair.
Her tail split in two.
Soon you'd never have known
she wasn't my wife.

Our love-making grew intense,
her mouth surging over me.
She would sigh, toss her head,
her hair storming the pillow,
body lifting like a wave, sometimes.

I became content with her – ten years,
slept easy in her arms
till I woke to an unlatched door,
the moon spilling in.
I ran bare-foot over rock
found her naked in the water, the stars
scaling on her back.
She called out to me,   opening her arms,
but I couldn't swim and was afraid,
afraid of the wild joy in her eyes,
her ten years inside.

She splashed back into the moon,
scattering it, coiling herself in its cool
till her body shone green.
In a flick she was gone,
leaving me to sail my boat,
a gull thrown back on the wind.

The Morning After

The look in her eye helped me recall it,
as I lay exhausted in the cream sheets of her bed.
Rest, she said.
The sun was cart-wheeling through the windows,
slamming off the white walls, the furniture.
My back was saddle-sore,
my knuckles, raw-red.

I remembered how the moon bounced
along the tree-line, how the road kicked back
behind me as I sped, slicing the air
with the bullet of my face,
my muscles full of the journey's song,
my heart, loud as a laugh,
keeping time in my ears.

And before that, tumbling out of bed in the dark
with my fingers clenched,
my fists hardening, my toes fusing into hoof,
spine stretching back and my neck arching.
I remember the walls of the room like a cage,
the need to burst through wind,
to pound the road, the earth,

and the look in her eye
when I stamped and turned, tossing my head
against the lacy frill of her lampshade,
causing light to dance,
wink off the gilt handles of her wardrobe;
lick a shine up her long black riding boots,
and her voice, husky, *Easy, easy, my love.*

Escalator

Hold me she asked,
turning on the escalator,
against the cold
and he wrapped his arms about her
hesitantly,
embarrassed someone might see
his arms around this woman
descending the escalator
into the city.
But his arms
took on a will of their own
as her head nestled like a bird
under his breast bone
and her hair-tips teased
his interlocked fingers.
He held her tenderly,
a boy with a fledgling,
his heart counting the seconds
till the escalator would slip
like a knife
under the footpath,
his arms fall away
and his eyes watch her
walk off into the city.

Hand

She lays her palm flat on a page of my jotter
and starting from the wrist
draws around the edge.
She tears out the page,
folds it into a small fist of paper.
Put it in your pocket, she says,
and I do,
walking all day through town
till the evening glow of street lamps
takes me to my own front door.
When I touch it then,
it slowly uncurls,
opens out into my hand.

Touch

Nothing is smooth:
not the spin in your skin
of its atoms,

not the star-dashed sky.
The lump and bump of a flat field
is revealed to the sole of a shoe.

You can see this with your fingers,
touch the centre of things,
sense their give and take,

their strain and breaking point.
The tree slowly pushing out its bark
has its own rough story to tell:

things crack.
You can feel them argue and snap.
They could splinter your head; your heart.

Better to open your eyes, go blind.

Drenched

The roads have cornered our park,
all colour has fled,

houses are humped, trembling,
against the back of the sky,

the pavements suddenly darkened –
rain sheeting down,

beating there like a sick pulse,
wanting in, getting under the skin.

I remember how you once slept in my arms
when I played you a recorded thunderstorm,

how you softened to a girl.
Gutters pool. Cars go blind. Water rants.

There is no argument can be made against it.
I wrapped you, that first time, in my coat,

your hair streaming, your body testing my banks.
The air is drowning. The sun has shut its eye.

And then, that last time, though I didn't know it,
when up on your toes, arms around my neck,

your sex burned against me.
Grey teems, fills the space between buildings.

Light-knives wound the sky. It rattles its lid.
Here is the room

where we held the clock from its tick.
Now, curtained small, it can't even hold out the dark.

There is no stopping the rain.
Our sun rusts under the hill.

Bat

It clung like a stain on the curtain
or closer, a kiwi fruit
absorbing all light on its skin.

I remember the stop of your fright when you saw it,
showing me into the bedroom,
how tight your smile.

Holding my breath,
I tapped it into a mug,
trapped there like a beating heart

which I flung from the window
and watched arc down, fold itself small
on the dangerous ground.

I turned back to the room
where my bags sat slumped on the floor.
You were still poised in the doorway

as if ready to pull back,
close yourself out,
should I make one mistake.

Bother

Does it bother you, she asked,
that I keep saying 'I love you'
all the time?
The park was a quiet afternoon,
autumn was waning.

I remember her breast brushing my arm –
Hail Mary full of grace –
as she half-turned, side-stepping,
to look into my face
and the wind whipping up the darkness.

Soon it would rain
and there'd be no place to stand or lean
without getting wet.
Her lips were under my coat,
her hand in my pocket.

I never answered.

But, yes, it bothered me. After.
When the only one in my coat
was myself,
when the park was too far to walk
and the days too dark.

The Field

The field still curls itself
round behind the hill
where I used to take her

to lie, hidden from the road,
close as two blades of grass,
her body scalding through her dress.

Now, twice the age,
I try to find her –
some remnant of the light perhaps

that holds the gleam of her hair –
but I cannot conjure her up,
just a vague sense of connection

and I wonder if this isn't all:
a boy, a field and a girl;
the road coming and going.

Falling

Love fell upon her like snow,
settling and building,
bright. She shone,
a CD disk fresh from its box.
Each day sang to her like a choir.

It wasn't that she was young
or didn't know the way seasons melt
one into the other.
It was just that she wanted to believe
in the whiteness of falling.

Secrets

When love was a secret
we kept it.
We were our own society,
hand seeking hand under cover.

The hiding place was the head
and the door was the heart,
the password we held
for that phone call late in the night.

When love was a secret –
invisible, need-to-know –
we followed its code,
meeting only in coffee shops, parks,

booking into hotels in late afternoon
and closing the blinds.
When love was a secret
it was tops. But it blew us apart.

Now that it's out
you have hung up your cloak
and only the dagger is left
in the who-done-it dark.

Ordnance Survey Ireland 84 – West Cork

Hungry Hill, Derryclancy, Coombane –
high names in her silent room,
his dinner cold on the table,
the clock slowly wiping its face –
Claddaghgarriff, Knockowen, Rams Hill.

The quiet life. The long tick of the room.
And now this unfolding
of an old map, the wood grain
stain of a mountain range,
her finger touching each town.

The moon is loud on the road;
her right hand cold on the pane,
frozen like five points of a star
when she reached out to his falling.
Now he sways at the gate, singing.

In her other hand the mountains
are folded away – West Cork –
the breadth of the Irish sea
between the one hand and the other.
The names are packed in her head:

Rams Hill, Knockowen, Claddaghgarriff,
Coombane, Derryclancy, Hungry Hill.

Journeyman

I open the map on the bonnet,
smooth its creases, line up a hill, a church,
travel the road with my fingertip
till the wind flaps it up.
I fold it away with the road held in my head –
two miles to the railway bridge, turn left.

I'm never lost with a map, my head full of journeys,
all waiting on the turn or straight of a road
my mind will follow, so that here,
where the frayed edge of the sea
tatters itself on a shingle beach,
there's a road back to a place,

a window set over a table
where I sit in silence looking out
on a field filled with light and rain,
the slowness of cattle;
a road too, to a boy, his calm eyes wide
on his first view of the world,
first of my own in my arm, perfect,
now walking beside me,
twenty-four and strong and the same;

roads too to houses and times –
my sister's house on a hill
where she tells of water coming up
where the hazel wand dipped,
clear and clean, tasting of stone,
and how once the field was black with crows,
that rose as one on her,
a dark blanket slapping into the sky,
fright she'd forgotten until the telling;

and my father stepping back from a door
and I standing into a room
where my dead brother has gathered the neighbours;
my mother too, about her daily ceremony,
singing brightness into the room
before turning to scoop me up from my cot.

All these like the dots of towns
held in place by their web of roads
and I, always coming home in my head,
taking every road back.

Rooks

for Rosemarie

They line up on the telegraph wire,
old newspaper hacks
in their lived-in suits,
rakish in their ragged blacks,
undertakers giving you the side-eye
as you stand out onto your path.

The days are changing. You step
so as not to jolt your back.
Two years on and still the ache of impact
deep in the twist of soft tissue,
in the unsure ballast of bone.

The morning is bright and you can see
as far as the mountains, the sun
on a hay field, a white-washed barn.
You remember yourself as a young girl
with the wide sea of a summer
between one schoolroom and the next.

You shake your head.
The rooks lift in unison,
a dark sheet flapping over the yard.
The world tilts
as if it might tip you out of yourself

and for a moment, you are back in your car
watching the cab of an articulated lorry
rise up in your rear-view mirror,
a dark lord opening his embrace.

Tír ná nÓg

is to stand up onto a doorstep,
lift the weight of a brass knocker,
hold it, then let it fall
booming into the house,

to wait there with my father
for the door to open
on granny shining out from the hall,

to cross into that cathedral of cool,
daddy closing the door
on the heavy world
and hanging his years on a peg,

following down the soda-bread air
to a boy's kitchen,

eager to be fussed over,
to have bread hot and yellow with butter,
milk cold from the fridge,

to watch my father on his tiptoes
at his mammy's elbow
stirring the creamy mud of a cake-mix

or sitting on her knee,
the radio humming
and I melting my bread on my tongue,
the white kiss of milk on my lips.

A Matter of Time

for Fergus

Sometimes it just slips away.
You can't even reach out.
You just watch it go,
dragging that vast silence in its wake
like the monstrous moment
after a door slam;
a slap in the face.
Look, you have known this all along.
It was a ship and an iceberg,
a match ripping itself
along an emery board: just
a matter of time.

But you got here. This far.
If you hadn't of stayed with it
you'd still be back in your box
with your bucket and spade.
Too far now to be safe,
you're out on the ocean
dreaming up a storm.
But look again – those are your arms
cutting into the waves,
those are your shoulders
rising like small question marks
out of the dark.

My Father's Greatcoat

My father's greatcoat was double-breasted, brown,
rough tweed that would make me pull back
if he drew me too close. The large belted buckle
was like a small door he kept locked,
the two rows of buttons like sentries.

The pockets had flaps and were empty
except for the times when his brothers would treat him
or there was money to spare for a dark bar
of Mick McQuaid plug that he'd pare into a pouch
with the smallest of penknives.

I liked to watch the attention he paid
to packing the bowl of his Peterson pipe,
the way he sucked the flame of a match
through that pipe deep into himself. Once
I threaded the stem of a buttercup through the buttonhole

on the left lapel, found excuses to open the door
of our under-stairs cloakroom, through an arc of dark,
so my eye could catch its little wink of light.
But next morning there was nothing,
just the shrivelled droop of it that I brushed to the floor

before my father came down.
And one other time, on a night when stars
seemed to be crying out from the cold
and the road home from granny's
made my legs bump into each other,

the arms of the coat scooped me onto its shoulder
where the bite of the tweed on my cheek
somehow felt safe
and I could watch my father's heels
flick out from its hem, then slip silently under.

Frames

i

We are in our small square kitchen
laughing with daddy
who sits enthroned in his corner
beneath the blue and gold of Our Lady;
the shelf with his rack of Peterson pipes,
his books – *Electrical Engineering,*
The Imitation of Christ.
The radio crackles a jig
and the shine on his boot winks
as he reaches out for mammy,
pulls her onto his knee.
We are all caught in this extravagance –
my plump mother bounced,
her face flushed, pushing herself up, *Tommy!*
her mouth cross, her eyes dancing.

ii

I leap the banisters,
landing crouched as a wrestler in the door-frame.
Daddy, red-faced, stands with his belt fisted,
my young brother in the vice of his other hand.
His anger is a great moment of silence.
I notice the tremor in his shoulders;
the power in his face.
My skinny frame challenges his bulk.
My head is somewhere else
watching myself circle and shout,
my own hands balled, my chest tight.
So you're old enough now? he challenges,
blocking the door as I take my brother's hand.
Yet he steps back from the fight and I pass
thinking somehow that I've won.

iii

Daddy came home to his mother
in the brown of a Franciscan friar's habit
to kneel in bare-sandaled feet
by his father's death bed.
Eldest of six, he stayed on
as provider, apprentice electrician,
in steel-toed boots. Hating it.
Years later he showed me
the soft white length of rope he'd kept
coiled on the back shelf of his wardrobe
like a snake tempting his return
to a cloister's silence. He held it up between us
in his wide-opened palms.

Garden

I watched
as Daddy sunk an ornamental pond,
laid a patio and then
a twist of path
between shrubs and flower bed,
on clean white paper.

Each summer saw me
safari through high grass,
flatten out a space
to lie back under blue.

At seventeen I took a scythe
and thrashed the green stalks low.
Mammy watched me sweating from the door
but never said a word.

Man on the Moon

My father went to the moon
and left me
in our end-of-terrace house
with its chest-high garden grass,
its clothes-line pole that wobbled
and a bedroom full of brothers,

he went to the moon
and I stood in the garden at night,
looked up and wondered
if he was looking down,
if he dreamt of my sisters and mother,
of me and my brothers sleeping
in our large back bedroom,

looked up at the pebble-dashed sky
trying to imagine the face of my father,
a stout man in a spacesuit,
his cardboard suitcase grasped
in his gauntleted hand,
his oxygen strapped to his back,

looked up and blinked the stars from my eyes,
blinked him a message in Morse
that it was time it was over,
that he should put the moon behind him,
shake its dust from his boots
and arrive by rocket, plane or parachute,
stand there beside me
and name me the names of the constellations.

Expurgatory

After I'd swallowed the house and moved on,
my father came to the door and opened his arms.

It seemed to me, looking into myself, that he sang
like a bird puffing out its chest at the dawn.

Then he went in and the click of the lock,
off-beat as it was, stuttered my heart.

All day at my desk, and at lunchtime walking the street,
my attention coiled inwards, to beat

at the door he had closed, my eye at the slit
in the curtains, my fingers plunging my throat,

wanting it out, the kitchen table before me,
my father lifting the pot and filling my cup.

How It Could Happen

It could be an evening like this,
turning away from a mirror,
the garden moving closer to the house,
the lights not yet lit,
that the corner of my eye will catch him
glancing at me from the glass
before slipping aside, gone
when I step back in front.

Or perhaps early,
the sun not up, I'll be in the kitchen
filling a cup at the tap
when the room will momentarily darken
and I'll sense a shape at the door
till I turn and the room brightens,
the sky lying against the door glass,
blond, blazon, the morning risen.

But I'll know he's been there,
trying to find a new language
of light and shade, some way to bridge the gap,
leave some message,
or maybe just to reach out,
the way the wind might move through a room
to turn the pages of a book,
brush the sleeves of a coat in the hall.

This is how it could happen.
This way or some other.

Everything

Now everything has gone –

>   the moon with its cold music,
>   the slow white of the snow,
>   the small turning of the leaf in the dark,
>   the gate closing in on itself,
>   the dustbin with its fat laugh,
>   the buzz of the last van in the distance,
>   the distance,
>   you.

>   There are books on the table,
>   all the pages torn.
>   The words have burned through the covers
>   and smoulder on the floor.

Now everything has gone –

>   the trees with their tattered leaves,
>   the birds with their crooked smiles,
>   the sky that sat at the top of the steps,
>   the coin in the gutter,
>   the bicycle leaning on its shadow,
>   the horizon's accident in the distance,
>   the distance,
>   you.

>   See how the water calls.
>   There is such room under the waves.
>   You could go down into it like the sun
>   and never be cold again.

Now everything has gone –

       the wall with its vertical pain,
       the little hooks of the wind,
       the rustle of children in the park,
       the dark,
       the road's irresistible urge to travel,
       the creak of the stars as they shift their geometry,
       the galaxy,
       you.

The Grandfathers

My father's father went into the mountains
to bring messages to the boys on the run.
My mother's father put a gun against his shoulder
and shot a guard on the road out of town.

He was with a band of men marching to Dublin
to join up with Connelly in the GPO.
My father's father did door-to-door insurance,
he knew all the hidden places where the boys laid low

and the drop points for a parcel or a note.
He asked no questions but collected his shilling at each door
then went on about his business. My mother's father
spent four years in Kilmainham jail, wore

himself out swapping cheese for cake
with De Valera, till the Free State got him out
to drink himself senseless on a bar stool
buying pints and chasers for every rogue and lout

who'd call themselves comrades, cosy up beside him
while his wife put the children to bed
before taking herself weeping into her own arms.
This is where I started, when all is done and said:

taking every road out of that countryside,
glancing over my shoulder at the dead.

One Frozen Winter

two swans remained in the shuck behind our house,
out of injury, maybe, unable to escape.
They learned to depend on my mother
for bread dipped in warm milk, left-over vegetables.
Daddy showed me how to feed them crusts from my palm
and keep my fingers safe.
In the hectic run up to Christmas, my mother forgot
till the tap of a beak on the door admitted one bird,
then its partner, steering the massive boats of their bodies
between chair and table, sailing into the kitchen,
crossing that border between outer and inner,
between wild and tamed, waiting for us to play host to them
there in the sanctuary of our own kingdom.

Years later, Daddy too crossed into a new kingdom
walking home from Mass
in that suit whose knees he'd worn to a shine,
between one footstep and the next,
slamming the footpath with the full weight of his body –
a knocker hammered down against a door –
his head cracked and bruised under the makeup
when I saw him laid out later at home,
his hands softly folded without a scratch,
and he off in some other kitchen, I like to think,
sailing in like a swan or
the way snow rises up on the back of the wind
and then settles down.

Night

I pass hooded doorways, the opening mouth of the alley,
a slab of a wall with its back against the sky (the sky
with its fierce eyes). Here are passing places, portals,
touch-points, gaps in hedge or banked earth where the force
of the night is heavy.
                        It is here I come on my father,
leaning over the wall of a bridge. I know him by the sweet smell
of his pipe, the smoke that softens the air between us.
He is listening, it seems, to the slap of the water
as if for some message, some resolution.
                        He knows I am here but he says nothing,
keeps his back turned, as if to face me might change too much.

Carrying my Father

We took my father's coffin on our arms,
assured by the funeral director
that this was fine and showed no disrespect.
I would have held him high on my shoulder
but his brothers were getting on in years.
Facing each other we held him in our arms
and shuffled from the church out to the hearse.
Then, once more, from hearse to open grave.

We planted him in his glazed pine shell –
he held onto his silence, I held mine –
still as a seed in the dark settling soil.
Then I returned to England and my life.
My letter that had never made the post –
Dear Daddy, I'm coming home, burned:
there's no going home now to my father,
he's no more need for anything that's mine.

My Father's Suitcase

Sunday evenings, invariably late,
we walked to the station,
me lugging his suitcase, seeing him off,
his breath short from the long hill.

He would ask me to run,
tell the station master to hold the train.
Even then I knew
that the world ordered itself differently

and never wanted the weight of that task.
And the times I stood,
my sweat cooling, the train
pulling away at my back, case at my feet,

watching him chug himself onto the platform,
that look of dismay on his face,
so that I felt that my effort was less
than it should have been

and I wanted to give him the miracle
of a train panting, its doors still open. But instead
we would turn, start the slow walk home,
the heavy case in his hand.